Oceans and Seas

Red Sea

Tamara L. Britton
ABDO Publishing Company

visit us at
www.abdopub.com

Published by ABDO Publishing Company, 4940 Viking Drive, Edina, Minnesota 55435.
Copyright © 2003 by Abdo Consulting Group, Inc. International copyrights reserved in
all countries. No part of this book may be reproduced in any form without written
permission from the publisher.

Printed in the United States.

Photo Credits: AP/Wide World, Corbis

Contributing Editors: Kate A. Conley, Kristin Van Cleaf, Kristianne E. Vieregger
Art Direction & Maps: Neil Klinepier

Library of Congress Cataloging-in-Publication Data

Britton, Tamara L., 1963-
    Red Sea / Tamara L. Britton.
        p. cm. -- (Oceans and seas)
    Summary: An introduction to the physical characteristics and plant and animal life of
the Red Sea, which is located in the Middle East and is an arm of the Indian Ocean.
    Includes bibliographical references and index.
    ISBN 1-57765-990-2
    1. Red Sea--Juvenile literature. [1. Red Sea.] I. Title. II. Series.

GC741 .B75 2003
551.46'733--dc21

                                                                        2002028329

Contents

The Red Sea

The Red **Sea** is located in a region of the world called the Middle East. The Red Sea's waters separate the Arabian **Peninsula** from Africa. Many countries border the Red Sea. They are Yemen, Saudi Arabia, Jordan, Israel, Egypt, Sudan, Eritrea, and Djibouti.

The Red Sea has not always looked as it does today. Scientists believe that about 200 million years ago Earth had only one continent, Pangaea. Pangaea was surrounded by one large ocean, Panthalassa.

Over many years, Pangaea began to break into pieces. These pieces became today's seven continents. The continents slowly drifted across Earth, dividing Panthalassa into new oceans and seas.

Today, the Red Sea is part of the Indian Ocean. This long, narrow sea covers an area of 169,000 square miles (437,708 sq km). It is home to many different plants and animals.

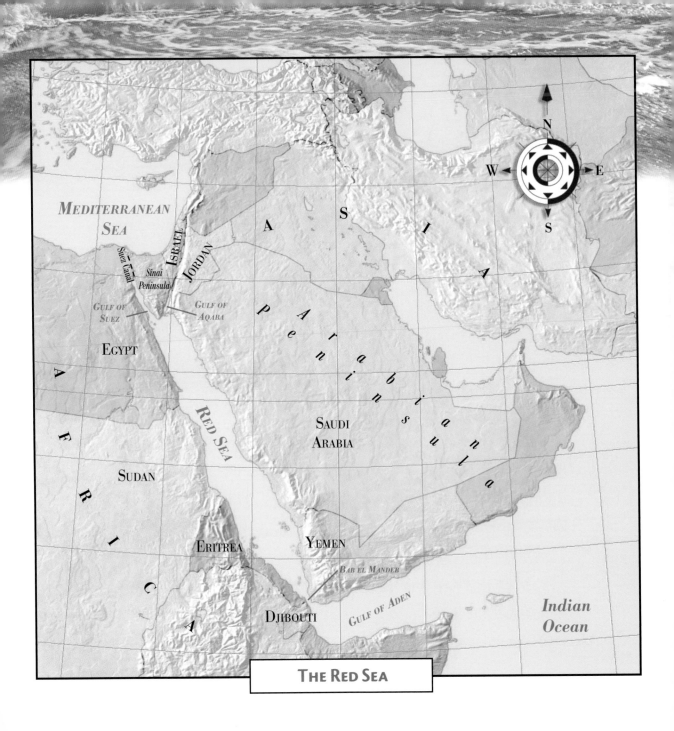

THE RED SEA

The Red Sea Begins

Earth's surface is divided into sections called plates. Earth's land and water sit on these plates. Beneath the plates lies **molten** rock. The plates float on this hot, liquid rock.

The Red Sea

About 35 million years ago, the African and Arabian Plates began to drift apart. Water from the Indian Ocean then filled the space between the two pieces of land. This area became the Red **Sea**.

Today, the African and Arabian Plates are still moving. The Arabian **Peninsula** is moving away from Africa. This movement occurs at a rate of about one-half inch (1 cm) each year.

The plate movement means the Red **Sea** is still developing. In fact, scientists believe the Red Sea is actually a young ocean that is growing. Scientists estimate that in 150 million years, the Red Sea might be as large as the Atlantic Ocean.

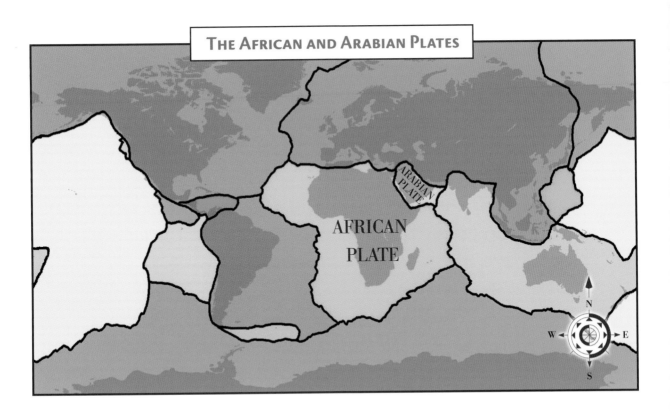

THE AFRICAN AND ARABIAN PLATES

7

Red Sea Geography

The Red **Sea** is a gulf of the Indian Ocean. The Indian Ocean is the third-largest ocean in the world. It lies between the Atlantic and Pacific Oceans.

The Red Sea connects to other bodies of water. In the south, Bab el Mandeb is the strait that connects the Red Sea to the Gulf of Aden. In the north, the Suez Canal links the Red Sea with the Mediterranean Sea.

The northern end of the Red Sea splits into two arms. The northeastern arm is the Gulf of Aqaba. The northwestern arm is the Gulf of Suez. The Sinai **Peninsula** separates these gulfs.

Most of the Red Sea is shallow. However, along the bottom of the sea is a central **trough**. It reaches depths of 7,000 feet (2,134 m). This central trough contains several **deeps**. Hot **brine** seeps up from these deeps into the Red Sea.

8

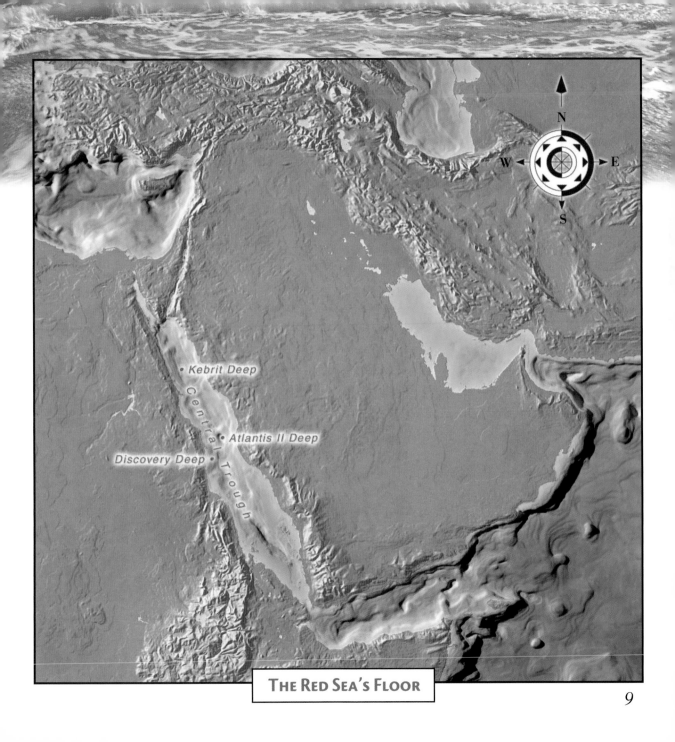

THE RED SEA'S FLOOR

The Red **Sea** lies in a desert region. Because of this climate, the air surrounding the Red Sea is hot. This keeps the Red Sea's water warm. In fact, the water's temperature a mile below the surface can reach 72°F (22°C).

Often, oceans and seas receive water from many different sources. However, the land near the Red Sea receives hardly any rain. And no rivers flow into the Red Sea. So the Red Sea's main source of water is the Gulf of Aden.

Water in the Red Sea evaporates as part of the hydrologic cycle. Normally, the evaporated water would be replaced by rain or rivers. But a lack of rivers and little rain mean the Red Sea's hydrologic cycle takes 20 years to complete itself.

Salt deposits form along the Red Sea's shore.

The Red **Sea**'s water is very salty. That is because the hot climate evaporates the water quickly. When the water evaporates, salt is left behind. With little fresh water entering the sea, salt builds up in the water.

THE HYDROLOGIC CYCLE

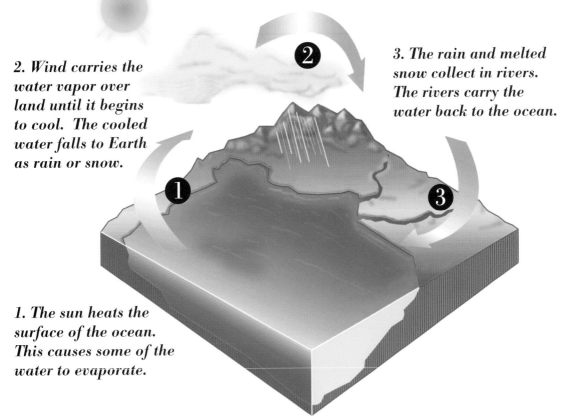

2. Wind carries the water vapor over land until it begins to cool. The cooled water falls to Earth as rain or snow.

3. The rain and melted snow collect in rivers. The rivers carry the water back to the ocean.

1. The sun heats the surface of the ocean. This causes some of the water to evaporate.

Plants

The Red **Sea** is home to many kinds of plants. Plants called algae grow well there. When one type of algae dies, the Red Sea's blue water turns reddish brown. This is how the Red Sea received its name.

Other plants live in the Red Sea, too. Eleven types of sea grasses grow there. They often live in shallow water near the coast. Sea grass beds are important because they provide food and shelter for many of the Red Sea's animals.

Mangroves also grow along the Red Sea. These plants live in the wet, salty soil close to the shore. Mangrove trees and shrubs have roots that grow above ground. The roots form **thickets** along the shore.

Opposite page: Green algae grow on a sponge in the Red Sea.

Animals

Many animals live in the Red **Sea**. The most important animals are coral. When coral die, their skeletons form large, beautiful **reefs**. These reefs are home to many other animals. The reefs also make the Red Sea a favorite area for scuba divers and snorkelers.

The dugong lives in the Red Sea's shallow waters. Each of these large mammals has two rounded flippers and a crescent-shaped tail. When dugongs rest in shallow water, they sometimes stand on their tails!

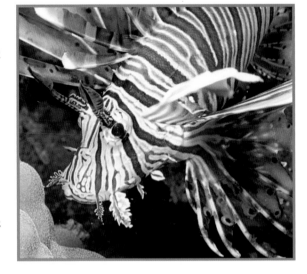

A lionfish

Many fish live in the Red **Sea**. Mako and hammerhead sharks, parrot fish, and puffers swim in its warm waters. Scuba divers and snorkelers must watch out for lionfish. Their sharp spines deliver a big sting!

Coral growing in the Red Sea

People

The Red **Sea** is in the Middle East. This region is often called the birthplace of civilization. People living on the lands bordering the Red Sea have made lasting contributions to the Middle East and the world.

Egypt is west of the Red Sea. Ancient Egyptians built the Pyramids and developed math, **geometry**, and **astronomy**. And, as early as 2000 B.C., Egyptians used the Red Sea as a trade route.

The Arabian **Peninsula** is east of the Red Sea. **Nomadic** tribes lived there. In the A.D. 600s, Islam began in this area. Today, Muslim **pilgrims** gather on the Red Sea's shores while traveling to **Mecca**.

Israel is north of the Red Sea. People have lived in Israel for 100,000 years. This ancient land is where the Jewish and Christian religions began. Today, this nation is home to people of many different faiths, including Jews, Christians, and Muslims.

Nomadic people, such as this Bedouin man, still live near the Red Sea today.

The Red Sea Today

Today, the Red **Sea** is a major transportation route. Ships moving between Europe and Asia can save time by traveling on the Red Sea. That is because the ships don't have to travel around the southern tip of Africa.

Each year, more than 1 million tourists visit the Red Sea. Its extensive coral **reefs** make it one of the world's best scuba diving locations. Tourists also visit the countries bordering the Red Sea. They visit historical and **cultural** sites, such as the Pyramids in Egypt and temples and shrines in Israel.

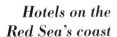

Hotels on the Red Sea's coast

Tourism and other human activities have affected the Red Sea. For example, people have built hotels, restaurants, and other buildings near the Red Sea. These construction projects cause soil **erosion**. They also hurt plant and animal **habitats**.

A scuba diver explores a coral reef in the Red Sea.

Oil tankers in the Red Sea

Human activities also pollute the Red **Sea**. **Desalinization plants** add chemicals and heat to the Red Sea. Fertilizers and pesticides used for crops run off into the sea. And in some areas, **sewage** enters the Red Sea.

As a result of human activities, the Red Sea's environment has been harmed. Many animals, such as the dugong, are endangered. Increased shipping traffic has damaged the coral **reefs**. And there is always the threat of an oil spill from one of the massive tankers traveling through the Suez Canal.

Today, Egypt is taking a lead role in preserving the Red Sea. Egypt has the Red Sea's longest coastline and most tourism. The country has made much of its coastline into national parkland and nature preserves. This keeps the Red Sea clean and healthy for the future.

The Red Sea along Egypt's coast

Glossary

astronomy - the science that deals with planets, stars, and other bodies in the heavens.

brine - water that is very salty.

culture - the customs, arts, and tools of a nation or people at a certain time.

deep - a long, narrow part of an ocean or sea that is more than 180,000 feet (5,500 m) deep.

desalinization plants - factories that remove salt from seawater.

erosion - wearing away of rock, soil, or land.

geometry - math that deals with points, lines, angles, and planes.

habitat - a place where a living thing is naturally found.

Mecca - an Islamic holy city located in Saudi Arabia.

molten - melted by heat.

nomadic - moving from place to place.

peninsula - land that sticks out into water and is connected to a larger landmass.

pilgrim - a person who travels to a holy place.

reef - a chain of rocks or coral, or a ridge of sand, near the water's surface.

sea - a body of water that is smaller than an ocean and is almost completely surrounded by land.

sewage - waste matter carried off by sewers.

thicket - an area with a dense growth of trees or shrubs.

trough - a long, shallow depression.

How Do You Say That?

algae - AL-jee
Aqaba - AH-kah-buh
Bab el Mandeb - BAHB-ahl-MAHN-dehb
Djibouti - jih-BOO-tee
Eritrea - ehr-uh-TREE-uh
hydrologic - hi-druh-LAH-jihk
Mediterranean - meh-duh-tuh-RAY-nee-uhn
Pangaea - pan-JEE-uh
Panthalassa - pan-THA-luh-suh

Web Sites

Would you like to learn more about the Red Sea? Please visit
www.abdopub.com to find up-to-date Web site links about the Red
Sea and the creatures that live there. These links are routinely monitored
and updated to provide the most current information available.

Index